Inspirational Poetry, Rhyme and Verse

On Life and Love

Emily Charlotte Harris

GW00498932

Inspirational Poetry, Rhyme and Verse

On Life and Love

Emily C. Harris

Compiled and edited by

Tycho Photiou

Inspiration

A flame that flickers slowly,
may soon become a fire,
One single human thought
a city can inspire.

Contents

PART TWO - ON LOVE

ON LIFE

A Small Tale

Once upon a time the earth,
no moon yet had it found,
Its seas unruly threatened
to swallow up its ground.

Lost in space amid the stars,
a tiny orb still wandered,
An orphan of our galaxy,
its power so truly squandered.

One night the earth
still searching for,
a ruler of its seas,
Spied the moon
far out in space
and captured it with ease.

Immortality

Here to stay in this space,
Our calendar of days,
This place we named the earth,
That age and death betrays.

But if we
climbed that mountain,
Where mist and sky abide,
And feel the tremor of the earth
against our soul collide.

From prophecy to ancient tale,
we'd understand this truth,
That nature knows of no
betrayal - of Life,
nor Love, nor Youth.

Counterpart To The Everglade

I've often thought
that we were made,
Counterpart to the everglade,
A vehicle to best convey,
that which nature
could not say.

She knew the folly of her deed,
when She grounded
the first human seed,
Long before we lived to prove
the irony of such a move.

But a smile still moves
her ancient gaze,
In the morning mist
or summer haze,

For what other creature
could contain,
The warmth of love
and chill of pain,

And so complete
her perfect plan,
With the passion that
is held in man.

Reflections In
The Everglade

And in the everglade,
where sun and shadow play,
There we find the dappled light
where nature has her say.

And all that shower
of pleasantry,
Are as moments that we give,
Reflected in the human heart,
Where both
light and shadow live.

Players

Confused as how
to play the game,
That comes with no instructions,
A game of life
where every answer,
Births a thousand questions.

But if we look beyond to where
Each riddle's an illusion,
We'll find 'tis only
our poor selves
That cause so much confusion.

15

The Dance

Oh this dance of life,
where does it lead us to?
Sometimes in step
with strangers,
Sometimes in step close to,
Sometimes we dance
in each other's hearts,
And sometimes
we haven't a clue.

Sometimes abroad
and sometimes at home,
Sometimes together
and sometimes alone.

16

But no step is dull,
And none without thought,
When again in life's music,
We find ourselves caught,

Steps that seem right,
Steps that seem wrong,
All we can do,
Is keep dancing on.

The Wheel Of Life

From East and West
we gather,
To question and to seek,
The adventurer, the scientist,
The spiritual and the meek.

Unhindered by
the mark of time,
The heart still marches on,
Searching, ever searching,
hopeful in it's song.

18

We name it Nirvana,
we name it Paradise,
We worship holy Trilogies,
we make our sacrifice.

But there are no conclusions
though we may live and die,
Can the answer lie
in a baby's cry,
before it can say I?

The "Trinity"

Breathing back into the "now"
No worry to displace,
The future, I shall let it be,
For life is not a race.

And I shall stand in "trust",
For centred there I'm free,
A strength that binds us
step by step,
To our destiny.

Each moment spun
within "loves" veil,
So gentle to each soul,
And from this trinity we step
unbound into this world.

The Best Game
In Town

When all the pieces that
have so carefully been placed,
And dreams and wishes
somehow with reality keep pace,

Never losing sight
of the reasons that we be,
Soft and warm,
Proud and strong,
Loving and so free,

And so again to bed, to dream,
   Of what to life we give,
   As slowly, very slowly,
Every dream we'll learn to live.

Life's Certainties

Did you know that
in all certainty there's doubt,
And did you know
the deepest love,
can turn us inside out.

And age can make us blind
to the child that lives within,
And every lie is waiting for
a truth to be let in.

And shadows only fall
when a distant light
glows bright,
And days are called to heel
by the spirits of the night.

And we are filled with dreams
that beg to be set free,
And every single moment
links us to eternity.

Returning

So delicate a web,
That truth itself shall weave,
No thought can interrupt it
on its course,
For all peripherals,
Complexities and masks,
Can only ever lead us back,
In footprints to its source.

The Chalice

The chalice bold dares to speak,
    Of higher there than I,
Aspirations where we reach,
    Imaginations spy.

The story teller that has been,
    Inside a dreamer's door,
    And speaks of tales
        therein, wherein
Each dreamer's passed before.

Thoughts/Reflection

And so another dreamer
Takes me by surprise,
Human fascination
Reflected in our eyes.

Elevated dreams,
Rising to each wish,
Magic in the making,
All we have and all we miss.

Nothing ever perfect,
Nothing so ideal,
But 'tis the dreamer's
dreams you'll find,
Ever spinning fortune's wheel.

By Accident
or Design

Mystified by past and future,
Is it all so random placed?
Or a human memory,
That's somehow been erased?

And could predictions be
already there designed?
Yet given leave
to change all things,
With the force
of the human mind.

The Human Legacy

I cannot take the clouds
upon my tongue,
Nor swallow whole the sky,
Nor can I package
up the stars,
Nor drink the river dry.

For all the beauty of this earth,
Our truest legacy,
Can never be possessed,
Yet still belongs to you and me.

Colour Me A-Mortal

Colour me a-mortal
who lived inside a time,
When clouds hung ripe
for plucking,
From an orchard sky.

And a generation grew
fresh bouquets of honesty,
And the naked flame of youth
burned the edges of hypocrisy.

And our teachers were
each other,
And the circles in a stream,
And music gathered in the air,
And settled in our dreams.

Across a bridge of memories,
Where love songs come to rest,
In a gentle page of history,
We carved a flower crest.

The Flower Crest
We Carved

A flower crest we carved
inside a book of history,
Gathers dust as years slip by
too fast for us to see.

Then one morning we awake
To find ourselves full grown,
Another generation
takes the space,
That once we'd known.

I hold the book and blow away
the cobwebs from its pages,
Flicking through
I find the truth
and wisdom of all ages,

Bringing us to "now" a place
we all are bound to find,
For the years are but a journey
on the ocean of all time.

Time Surrenders

The years that stretch between
us now, invisibly suspended,
Tricked by gentle elements,
so timelessly intended.

And how the bright sunshine,
lifts us to its alter,
We slip into
each others thoughts,
Lest our words should falter.

Life journeys stretch
before us now,
Some painful and some tender,
But in the space between us,
They find a sweet surrender.

Are Our Worlds
The Same?

You live life almost next to me,
Growing in this world with me,
Breathing the same air as me,
Both seeing what
we both can see.

From side to side,
Back to front,
Our senses run in line,
How is it then,
The world you see,
Is so different from mine?

The Ego

The ego's a soft ball
destined to prance,
Through the forest of passion,
where we're all so entranced.

The branch that swipes you
As you dreamily pass,
The mud puddle you
stepped in,
Well hidden by grass.....

But make no mistake
you will survive,
With twigs in your hair
and grit in your eye.

And just as you think
it can't get any worse,
Your toe stumps a rock,
and you hear yourself curse,

Then on the breeze
laughter reaches your ears,
Glancing around
for the devil who dares,
Mock your misfortune
when your ego's so bruised,
Still feeling the squelch
of mud in your shoes.

Then the wind changes
From the East to the South,
And clearly you hear now,
The laughter is near now,
God bless you it comes from
Your very own mouth.

41

Trouble At Mill

I rest in the crest
of a wave that just passed,
A gentle respite
from aggressions cold blast.

But place me again
in that line of fire,
And I fear I'm afraid
of what may transpire.

Though I try to perform
as I know I should,
'Tis just imitation
of where I once stood.

For where there was pleasure
now there is pain,
And where there was sun,
there's now only rain.

Friendship

What is a friend but they,
Who tenderly hold
the best of you,

When for a while
your spirit,
Has been tossed into the blue.

A Simple Belief

When my eyes are tight shut
and its too dark to see,
My Angel he comes
with candles for me,

When all is confusion
and I can't understand,
My Angel he comes
and takes hold of my hand.

Guardian Angel

Anger was the fire that rose,
and scorched with every word,
In my soul I cried for help
and you my Angel heard.

And when I fell
and could not hide,
You moved in close,
there by my side,

And when the tears
began to fall,
I knew the greatest love of all.

You sent me gifts
of love so true,
Through friendship's guise,
from those I knew,

You gave them words
to give to me,
And bound me to them tenderly.

And when in time
they'd given all,
You braced me for
the final call,

As still that mile
I had to tread,
Truth pounding there
inside my head.....

Confined in fear of consequence,
While flames still leapt
from power's pretence,
You'd given me so much so far,
I had no choice
but drain the jar.

And so in trepidation's cloud,
I shunned the fear
and felled the shroud.

While you stood by,
though I couldn't tell,
'till words of truth
from my lips fell,

And cut through lies
with gentle force,
While angers wounds
felt pains remorse.

The truth at last
had reached its home,
This battle, I'd not
fought alone.

So how then can it ever be,
That pain should take
the best of me?
When I have such
a friendship true,
It's time now that
I fought for you.

The Rescue

I thought,
if only I were smart,
I could avoid this battle,
A daily fight
to do what's right,
As leader or as chattel.

To be too nice or stand aloft,
I chose not this endeavour,
Knowing that either one,
is not so very clever.

But oh the somewhere
in between,
The morsels thrown aground,
The smiles
and kindred whispers,
The times you come around.

The words like playthings
that we use,
In jest or most sincerely,
Come so timely to my ears
and rescue me completely.

Truth

Truth is pure, a feather white,
carried on the air of life,
Tossed, rebuffed,
refused, disguised,
Called a lie, it still survives.

Sticks And Stones

And after anger come the tears,
  like a waterfall so blinding,
And each of us then put away
the stones we kept for grinding.

"'Tis The Little Things That Count"

Human gesture so small,
How can you be measured,
Allow me to take from you,
all that I pleasure.

Insignificant scene
so naturally posed,
Allow me to be
to your essence exposed.

And when all so normal
a day passes by,
Allow me to hover
beneath the same sky,

And look on as a poet,
When tears become words,
At the wonder of all,
When through truth is observed.

For the eye that can see,
Beyond the mundane,
Will uncover the beauty,
Of all that seems plain.

And all that's confounded
By clarity caught,
And all that is grounded
Be winged by a thought.

Life

Running wild, running free,
All nature's gifts
you bring to me.

Spirit, soul, heart and mind,
A need to give, return in kind.

These awesome
treasures overflow,
From East to West,
where'er I go.

And all uncertainties dissolve,
From North to South
in purest gold.

The simplest truth
encaptured there,
'Tis only love
can match this fare.

ON LOVE

The Brave
Dare Fall

From the planets we fell down,
Naked to this earth,
Unknowing of our mission,
Unsure of our rebirth,

And some they played,
And others cried,
Some raised their eyes above,

Some they fought,
And some they dreamed,
But the brave they fell in love.

Insatiable Cupid

Insatiable Cupid,
Dreamer's delight,
Go fire your arrows,
into the night,

So silent, so swift,
How they tremble and fall,
Caught on a breath,
You stir and enthral.

Cupid such mischief,
You make with our hearts,
No one is safe,
When your arrow imparts.

We have no defences,
Will you never rest?
The pain and the pleasure,
How can we resist?

Love In Focus

When love comes in
and breaks the seal,
That held so fast through time,
It leaves a gentle legacy,
unsimple to define.

For how can we
describe the power,
Of that we cannot measure,
And how can we
explain the depth,
Of such a boundless pleasure?

Small as we are
in flesh and bone,
And frame so well deceiving,
Of that emotion flying far,
beyond the space we're living.

The Road

So many folk, so many smiles,
So much I have been given,
And I have choked
upon goodbyes,
When by life again I'm driven.

And been content to travel on
this, my road so free,
Until you came across my path
and walked a while with me.

64

And how you teased
And how you charmed,
And how you pained me so,
And how you climbed
into my soul,
I swear I'll never know.

The Model

And so
the inward silence spoke,
Invisible the shield and yoke,

And where my stories
tale began,
From each sonnet
there you sprang.

You who were Achilles wrath,
And I the pilgrim artist lost.
And you Narcissus in repose,
Yet 'twas I, who was exposed.

How and when
shall Titian rise,
From these hands
and from these eyes,

To do such justice
to your flesh,
That lights and falls
in shadowed mesh.

While Hercules
more brave than I,
Shall mock from his
Olympian sky,
And will the Gods there,
glance upon,
The plateau you and I
stand on.

The Photograph

Strong hands on my shoulder,
An image lost in time,
Reflections of our destiny,
Past and future, undefined.

Two souls bound and captured,
'Cross a canvas in my mind,
One night I whisper to you:
"We belong somewhere
in time".

Beauty Beheld

What master carver sculpts
the dearest faces that we love?
Whose beauty makes us
gentle ache,
And fits our vision
hand in glove.

Caught in our sight
we're everywhere,
We ever wish to be,
But then you leave
and take with you,
a tiny part of me.

The Affair

The Artist,
she could not at first discern,
His eyebrow raised
in vague concern.

Candles lit
their introductory scene,
Canvas stained in colours,
where his life had been.

She thought herself
modestly wise,
'till he lay her naked
with his eyes,
And left her shamefully little
to disguise.

And in a Jutted memory
the candles burn,
He said
that he would teach her,
if she should return.

And in a dream of dreams,
she let her inhibitions fall,
Hung her cloak
of independence in the hall.

Let slide her single sheet,
slippery to the floor,
And returned to know again,
the welcome at his door.

The Scene

You star in my life
far too fondly I'm sure,
And if you but knew
its all happened before,

Another lead role
on a heaven lit stage,
Written and cast
at the turn of a page.

Another stage kiss,
another encore,
Changing the scene and the
musical score,

While cupid he teases
and smiles from the wings,
And again I am dancing
to the sweet song he sings.

The Meeting

We gathered there
in casual air,
One night
when day was through,
Life and love so closely tied,
the likes of me and you.

Then you came by
and I watched your words,
paint pictures of my dreams,
Matching every image
that my heart had ever seen.

I dared not speak,
nor draw a breath,
As your voice reached
to my soul,
That night when two halves
of a dream,
Together became whole.

Words And Moments

In just a few moments,
so welcome and warm,
Conceived on the air,
again truth was born,

Uncovered and shameless,
naked and prone,
As a young colt released,
to find its way home.

From our souls
came its secrets,
In whispers and sighs,
And tears overflowed
in the absence of lies.

And if ever a wish
was a wish meant to be,
It's that truth shall survive
between you and me.

Secret Garden

When I first entered
deep your smile,
Impatient to explore,
I knew that only time could lift
the latch on every door.

I didn't want to trespass,
where I should not tread,
But you took my hand and
through your secret garden
I was lead.

Yet Unwritten

Two years the Author's
quill has laboured,
Between untitled covers,

Uncertain still
to make these two
Be friends or transient lovers.

Destiny's Choice

Well my little Angel
So you do or do not come,
One will see my spirit rise,
The other spill tears in my eyes.

And if I could
make things thus,
I would bring you here,
but then,
Which of us has the power
to guide the Author's pen?

Fate Changes
Its Mind

Edit plans written in,
Who can tell on a whim,
What goes out must come in,
Reconciled faith within,
Changing all
that may have been,

For the wider concept known,
To only those and those alone,
Who in their wisdom do exhale,
A truth that fashions
each detail.

Windows To The Soul

The voices of so many souls,
Find refuge in the eyes,
Calling to each other,
Through their veiled disguise.

Swimming there
In pools of light,
By word nor action tethered,
Transcending every falsehood,
Where each lie
by truth is severed.

And chance then finds us
locked in space,
One time and so completely,
And through our eyes
the song of souls,
Sings to our hearts so sweetly.

Unrequited Love

He, I know, would never want
to cause me hurt nor harm,
He who little knows my heart
rests warm inside his palm.

He who all the rules of love
would so easy break,
Holds fast to this
true friendship,
For our friendship's sake.

And I have been so hasty,
and blind to understand,
That this our true alliance,
'Gainst time
shall long withstand.

And should I trip and stumble
O'er this truth I cannot tell,
He will, with cheer,
lift me back up,
Never knowing why I fell.

Soaring Spirit

Oh soaring spirit
that needs to burst,
Into the space around me,
Searing flames that leap inside,
why do they so confound me?

I have no real
control save thought,
Which each emotion tests,
But oh how much
I yearn for these
emotions to find rest.

Inside your door
and at your feet,
And 'gainst your heart
be pressed,
There to spill each drop of love
for you that I possess.

Winged Words

In the crowded smoky air,
my heart to yours was calling,
You brushed away a single tear
that on my cheek had fallen,
For all the things
I could not say,
my lips from silence swollen.

And you weren't meant
to know the why,
Of such impulsive drama,
But then your touch,
peeled away,
my final shred of armour.

And 'mid the noise
I sent to you
A truth I could not fight,
And tenderly you caught it
like an injured bird in flight.

Paradise

You fell from my sight
for just a short span,
How I missed you, not knowing
it was part of the plan.

I tried so in vain
to believe in the whole,
But that empty space
my paradise stole.

And I was so pained
I misunderstood,
That all that took place,
took place as it should.

And then you returned
with so much you had planned,
And gently placed paradise
back in my hand.

Piece Of Heaven

Palms to the wind
is where I stand,
While love exhumes my heart,
And I shall tell you truly,
On my breath
where words depart.

And travel where the desert sun
rests upon the sand,
To seal a vow
that memory holds,
Precious in her hand.

And if this vow
you chance to hear,
On the air of silence driven,
Your heart may know
in innocence,
My tiny piece of heaven.

A Special Bond

Caught up, strung out, in pain,
and so beside yourself,
As another lover lifts you up,
and dumps you on the shelf.

And you ask me how I feel
as I stand quietly by,
Watching you fall in and out
of love, I cannot lie.

For I shall be with you as long
as we still laugh and cry,
As long as truth
echoes between us,
And time keeps passing by.

And I'll stand next to you
while we share
each other's dreams,
And always know that
what we have,
Is much more than it seems,

So don't question what I feel,
when another lover sets you free,
Ask why on earth,
after all this time,
You're still
standing here with me.

The Kiss

Outside we stepped
on an idle whim,
The winters night so welcoming.

We had no right,
To steal that diamond
from the night,

But oh how
the stars they teased,
And would that we
their souls appeased.

Leaning close,
no thought in mind,
Bodies lightly
touched in time,

And then
the sweetest kiss became,
With only the starry
night to blame.

Anticipation

Dancing with stars
in their eyes,
Attractions hardly disguised,
Ever bolder as night runs away,
Excitement keeps
tiredness at bay.

Slippery intentions
upon the fun slopes,
Affections fly free,
elevating our hopes,
Anticipation comes out to play,
Tonight there'll be nothing
hidden away.

Only A Wish

Just for now be my Cupid,
my Hero entranced,
Be my Angel, my Lover,
my Music, my Dance,

Just for a while
let this symphony play,
Let's be bold, let's be brazen,
let's go all the way.

Seduction

When you breathe in the air
next to mine,
The delicate orb of the day
is defined,

And surrounds perfect space
seductively spun,
From that primal longing
where the brave are undone.

And if your gentle touch
in passing be won,
Sensations rejoice at the place
where you come,

And energies children
race to the scene,
For the firework display
where your hand has just been.

Deep Blue World

Skin to skin our bodies press,
Deep into the nights recess,

Ragged breath and milky eyes,
In a deep blue world we rise.

Silently where secrets kept,
Inside my very soul you crept.

Coming now,
the Dawning sweet,
Inside our deep
blue world complete.

The Morning After

A library, all oak
and atmosphere,
Veils of hair sheltered my eyes,
The swell of feelings
well disguised.

I surfed deliciously,
Last nights honeyed memory,
While in and out of sleep
I'd lost,
Strange images into my head
were tossed.

And intermittently
I read the book,
I'd chosen to inspire,
Those dreams, those memories,
and all that I desire.

Winter Love Sonnet

Had I known I'd wait so long,
for the sweetness of this love,
I'd have brought
a sleeping bag,
A hat and perhaps some gloves.

If I had known
it would take so long,
To feel this much for you,
I'd have made full sure
I'd worn a muff,
On my nose that's turning blue.

If I knew so many years
would pass,
Before this very day,
I'd have counted fondly
every single, moment
'long the way.

And if it comes to nothing,
or if it comes to all,
I still would write each detail,
in detail, to recall,

An oh so charming chapter,
a-musing tale to tell,
Of when I slipped and tripped
and down
Loves slippery slope I fell.

A Summer Adventure

Where do we go from here,
Stood between
the Earth and sky?
Shall we sail the oceans,
And watch the dolphins fly,

Ride across the desert,
on camels sat astride,
Climb atop a pyramid,
And watch the Earth subside,

Or go in search of treasure
in caves of golden vein,
Walk barefoot
'neith the shady palm,
Bathe in forest rain.

And if we should dive,
through coral reefs,
Of sunspilt silver light,
Would you come play
and could you stay,
To lay with me the night.

Letting Go

As love has bound
my heart full sore,
So too has made me wings,
That this strange place
I should explore,
And take what'er it brings.

And if my heart should swell
with such a malady as you,
I'll try to dream
another dream,
That holds no thought of you.

And if by chance
your name should pass,
my lips one winter's day,
I'll board the ship of freedom,
and sail far far away.

The Sapling

One starry night upon my lips,
you planted me a dream,
Emerging in the moonlight
a sapling evergreen,

And the little shoot
became a plant,
And the plant became a tree,
And now my willow
sighs and weeps,
For a love that cannot be.

The Wave

Take the bit, feel the blood,
 Rise above the pain,
If this is real, if this is love,
 then I shall love again.

The highs and lows
 are just a wave,
That takes us on its crest,
To challenge every human heart
 that beats in every breast.

Years Gone By

It's only when
the day light flickers,
To a softer haze,
And lovers leave
upon the breeze,
And our hearts
are hurt and dazed.

And we resent the moonlight
in other people's dreams,
And find that all around us
life has ripped at every seam.

And good things are forgotten
and pillows hold our tears,
And nothing was for nothing
as we gaze across the years.

The cost of every friendship
was a heartbreak all its own,
The cost of every pleasure
was another mile from home.

Moonlight Whisper

She delved so far and deep,
into his impudence and favour,
Tripping over daydreams,
that his kisses
may still save her.

And in between
each thought and dream,
He enters uninvited,
Like the title of a poem
yet to be recited,

Still she holds on to that fire,
Which drives
her sweetest wishes,
While the moonlight whispers:
"Let him be,
the sea holds many fishes".

A Friend

Where there's life
there shall I be,
To follow far too eagerly,

Perhaps too blinded by its light,
Single minded there in flight.

Escapist or Idealist,
I may never clearly see,
But those windows
that were shuttered,
You opened up for me.

And wherever
freedom carries me,
It will whisper there
your name,
And though others may be
part of me,
Your place they'll never claim.

Loves Not
A Single Flame

If love be but a single flame,
that guides us,
And all the rest,
our journey's cloak
that hides us,

We set ourselves
to search in vain,
Desiring of that single flame,

When all around
a thousand candles glow,
But in our single-minded quest,
We miss the best
of life's exquisite show.

Other Ocean Books publications:

You Are What You Think   ISBN 1 902422 00 7

You Really Are Responsible   ISBN 1 902422 02 3

Inspirational Thoughts Vol 1   ISBN 1 902422 01 5

Inspirational Thoughts Vol 2   ISBN 1 902422 03 1

18 Pentrich Avenue,
Enfield, Middlesex.
EN1 4LZ.
Tel (020) 8350 9600

We are but hungry Angels,
fallen from the light,
Searching out the crevices,
doubting in our plight.
Feeding on each morsel,
hopeful for still more,
Senses straining on the leash
of all that was before.
But when all is left unspoken
and the breath of life sustains,
The ties of fear are broken
and silent wisdom reigns.

Emily C. Harris

ISBN 1-902422-04-X

9 781902 422046

£3.95

A Call to Be

by
Mary and Mark Fleeson

This second edition published by: Lindisfarne Scriptorium
Farne House, Marygate, Holy Island of Lindisfarne, TD1!
United Kingdom. www.lindisfarne-scriptorium.co.uk

ISBN 978 1 909041 27 1

10 9 8 7 6 5 4 3 2

British Library Cataloguing in Publication Data.
A catalogue record for this book is available from the British Library.
Typeset by Lindisfarne Scriptorium Limited.
Book production and preparation by Hand in Hand Solutions Limited.